To a Wonderful Father

Illustrated by John Overmyer, Tracy McVay,
Margaret Phillips and George Kauffman

Hallmark Editions

This is a father...
  strength and gentleness,
strong shoulders, comforting eyes,
  hands that could build a birdhouse
or make a kite or lift a child
     high, high, higher...

into a world of leaves and sunshine
    and a nest of robins,
quiet understanding, steady encouragement,
    unquestioning love.
        This is a father.

Doris Chalma Brock

A father always overlooks our faults,
    but never our needs.

Mary Dawson Hughes

God took the strength of a mountain,
   The majesty of a tree,
The warmth of a summer sun,
   The calm of a quiet sea,
The generous soul of nature,
   The comforting arms of night…

The wisdom of the ages,
    The power of the eagle's flight,
The joy of a morning in spring,
    The faith of a mustard seed,
The patience of eternity,
    The depth of a family's need....

Then God combined these qualities
    And when there was nothing more to add,
He knew His masterpiece was complete
    And so He called it — Dad.

Herbert Farnham

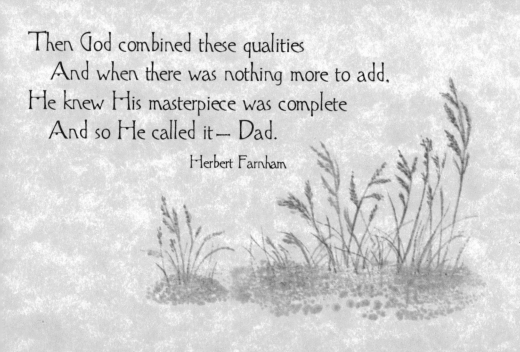

No one really understands just how a father knows
Exactly what a boy will need to guide him as he grows.
No one really understands the way a father can
Exactly what it takes to turn a boy into a man.

George Webster Douglas

Sometimes only a father is truly aware
Of his daughter's needs and wants and cares
And what she dreams and how she grows...
Sometimes only a father knows.

Marjorie Frances Ames

A dad remembers...
when no one else does.

Margaret Lindsey

A dad is a companion
Whose loyalty has no end.
For he's more than just a father...
He's the finest kind of friend.

Katherine Nelson Davis

No need to teach a bird to fly
Or teach a tree to touch the sky
Or teach the sun to shine above
Or teach a father how to love.

Robin St. John

What a father says to his children is not heard
by the world, but it will be heard by posterity.

Jean Paul Richter

A father guides with the gentle hand of love.

George Webster Douglas

Oh, what rich dividends it yields
To walk with dad in woods and fields;
To pause and rest in shady dells
Where Mother Nature's wonder dwells.
To simply wander here and there
And breathe the fragrant summer air.
To see a place where wild ducks nest,
And sunlight shine on mountain crest.

Then as the shadows gently fall
To hear a whippoorwill's soft call
    And watch a twinkling star respond
    To shine above the silvery pond.
Yes, every child is proud and glad
When he goes walking with his dad!

Reginald Holmes

No matter how many waves
   come rushing to the shore,
there is still another
   and yet one more.
Such is the love in a father's heart.

Tina Hacker

Happy the man who can leave his cares:
The stress of work and world affairs.
  To tramp about through the meadows and fields
  And enjoy the treasures that nature yields
    And feel its inspiration....

Happy the man who finds a place:
An interlude in time and space
   Where he can pause to muse and dream
   By a country lake or a mountain stream
      In quiet meditation.

Barbara Burrow

A home is built on dreams of the future,
memories of the past and the ever-present strength
of a father's love.

Gale Baker Stanton

Father! — to God himself
we cannot give a holier name.

William Wordsworth

A dad knows how to give his children good advice,
   but he also knows that his children need
to think things out for themselves
      and form their own conclusions.
There are times when they must do the talking,
   times when they can really use a friend
      who will just listen…and understand.

Edward Cunningham

This is the kind of man he is—
   His children run to meet him.
And the eyes of his wife are aglow with love
   As she stands at the door to greet him.

Mary Dawson Hughes

No man can tell whether he is rich or poor
by turning to his ledger.
It is the heart that makes a man rich.
He is rich according to what he is,
not according to what he has.

Henry Ward Beecher